HOMESCHOOLING

A Mother-Daughter Account on Why It Was a Success

USA TODAY BESTSELLING AUTHOR
ARLENE MCFARLANE
with
EDEN MCFARLANE

Homeschooling: A Mother-Daughter Account On Why It Was A Success, Copyright© 2020 by Arlene McFarlane

All rights reserved, including the right to reproduce this book in whole or in part in any form.

Digital ISBN: 978-1-9994981-4-6
Print ISBN: 978-1-9994981-5-3

Published by ParadiseDeer Publishing
Canada

Cover Art by Eden McFarlane

Formatting by www.formatting4U.com

CONTENTS

BOOKS BY ARLENE MCFARLANE i
ACKNOWLEDGMENTS iii
INTRODUCTION 1
WHY HOMESCHOOL? 5
WHAT OUR DAY-TO-DAY LOOKED LIKE 11
SPECIAL DAYS 41
HURDLES AND CRITICISMS 55
BLESSINGS 65
FREQUENTLY ASKED QUESTIONS 73
SOCIAL MEDIA LINKS 78
ABOUT THE AUTHORS 79

BOOKS BY ARLENE MCFARLANE

FICTION

THE VALENTINE BEAUMONT MYSTERY SERIES

MURDER, CURLERS & CREAM
Book 1

MURDER, CURLERS & CANES
Book 2

MURDER, CURLERS & CRUISES
Book 3

MURDER, CURLERS & KEGS
Book 4

MURDER, CURLERS & KILTS
Book 5

MURDER, CURLERS & KITES
Book 6
(Coming Soon)

ACKNOWLEDGMENTS

BY ARLENE MCFARLANE

To my husband, who first presented the idea to homeschool our children. You've been our rock and constant role model, demonstrating an unparalleled love for the three of us in hundreds of ways.

To our family and friends—homeschoolers and non-homeschoolers. Through the highs and lows, your genuine kindness was a breath of fresh air, and your undying support was the encouragement I needed. You will forever have a special place deep in my soul.

Karen Dale Harris and Noël Kristan Higgins, thank you for your editorial input and for assuring this book was ready to see the light of day.

To Eden and Hart, you were the best students a teacher could have asked for. Smart. Motivated. Respectful. With a dose of good humor, spirit, and a ton of heart. I'm blessed to be called your mother and delighted we took this journey together.

Finally, to God, for being ever faithful and for guiding us day by day. You live in my heart.

INTRODUCTION

If you're opening the pages of this book, you're obviously curious about what homeschooling is about on a more personal level. I'm a parent like you. I get it. We all want our children to grow into smart, ethical, well-adjusted adults who have much to offer this world. It's a huge decision to homeschool, and we want it to be the right decision.

Though I'd instinctively "homeschooled" our children, Eden and Hart, from the time they were toddlers—starting them on the piano, teaching them the alphabet, working side by side on creative projects—I took on the task of their more formal education for ten years. That experience is still one of my favorite topics, and I'm constantly moved when new moms ask if they can pick my brain on the subject.

At times, in fact, they've been so grateful for what I've shared, they asked if I have a book that they could read on our experience. They wanted to know everything: from what we did, to how I managed, to what our kids thought of being homeschooled. They wanted a trusted source, and they wanted to hear more.

That put the wheels in motion to write an account about what homeschooling was like for us. Now, more than ever, home education is a growing trend, and I'm eager to share our endeavor with you.

Before I homeschooled Eden and Hart, however, I wasn't familiar with this method of education. I certainly didn't know anyone who did it. One thing I did know, though, was that I didn't want to deny our family the joy of being with our children in those early years. I dreaded the idea of sending them away every day to a place for others to educate and influence.

I still recall how, after our children were born, I watched our neighbor's three young girls board the school bus each morning. The youngest, four at the time, was so tiny, she struggled to lift her leg up onto the bus's step, the weight of her knapsack pulling her back to the ground. This scene broke my heart, and I realized I couldn't bear to send our kids away at such a tender age to a place where I had no input on anything they learned or experienced.

My husband, John, and I had been given two bright, beautiful children, and as their mother, I wanted to do my utmost to fuel them with positive energy, give them opportunity and insight on how to think outside the box, and let them know that it was not just okay to be different from others: it was a gift to be treasured. Teaching them at home would make it possible for them to experience all this and much more.

To be clear, this book was not written to criticize other educational systems or those who send their children to school. But it also would not have been written if our homeschooling venture had been a failure.

There are dozens of 500-page comprehensive volumes on homeschooling that cover subjects from an array of teaching methods, to advice on specific programs, to costs and budgets. Reading *this* short personal narrative will be like talking to friends over lunch. You'll discover what was most significant to us about homeschooling and receive encouragement and support as you proceed on your own homeschooling adventure.

Whatever a child's age when you decide to homeschool, it's normal to wonder what that child is internalizing about this unique way of teaching. How do they feel about being taught at home? Particularly, how do they feel about *not* going to school?

When I approached our daughter, Eden, about co-authoring this book, she agreed that regardless of the number of how-to homeschool books available, that a genuine, personal account from a mother and daughter would be beneficial. As Eden recently graduated university with her master's degree in French and had been homeschooled until entering high school, I knew she would add value to this book.

In the coming pages, you'll see some of the setbacks we encountered, along with the benefits and ongoing blessings. Without being too egocentric, I'll even share some visuals of our activities. Okay, I had to slip in a few images to illustrate a point, right? My aim, however, is that you'll be inspired and use whatever you find worthwhile if you travel this path.

At the end, there's an FAQ page that will answer common questions and address concerns people ask us about.

I know you want the best for your children, and I congratulate you for considering this option. You don't need a teaching background, a B.A. in psychology, or credentials in social work to homeschool. All that is required is a loving heart, a commitment to do your best, and permission to make mistakes along the way. If this book—and our experience—provides vision to assist you on your journey, then we will have reached our goal.

Lastly, if you've perhaps been forced into a homeschooling situation temporarily because of unforeseen events and/or health and safety reasons, take your time and fully consider your options before making a long-term choice. Homeschooling is not for everyone, and I'm not here to hammer you on the head with it to convince you otherwise. Just know, this book was written to inspire parents in all circumstances. You may not see it now, but I assure you, this could be the most rewarding time in your life.

WHY HOMESCHOOL?

This book is an account of what worked for us and why we chose to homeschool. We weren't living in a time of global pandemic nor did we have children with special needs. We had other valid reasons—you might as well—that contributed to our decision to take on this endeavor.

Our journey began when our daughter was a toddler and our son was a newborn. My husband, a well-loved and respected teacher in the public-school system, presented the idea that we should homeschool our children.

I remember my eyes popping wide open and responding with, "You think we should *what?*" I mean, he was a teacher. Surely he wouldn't suggest anything other than a traditional education.

We had moved into a brand-new neighborhood a few years before, and a new school had just been built. Despite the heartbreaking bus scene I'd witnessed each morning involving our neighbor's girls, I'd figured this was the school Eden and Hart would attend.

John, having firsthand insight into the school system and being the most objective person I know, gave me three simple reasons why he thought we should consider homeschooling.

The first reason had to do with limited individual assistance in a large classroom. At home, it would be one-on-one with instant feedback and an efficient use of time. There would also be fewer interruptions and less social troubleshooting.

We didn't presume our kids would have difficulties in any area, but we still didn't want them to get lost in the crowd. Furthermore, if our children grasped concepts and learned principles easily, there'd be no need to hold them back. We could work at our own pace and schedule.

The second reason to homeschool our children was the same as the naysayers' argument for putting kids *in* school...for socialization. We had no intention of hiding or protecting our children from the world, but it was important for us to raise them with love and respect and for them to grow in an environment free of negative influences that might tear down their character.

In essence, we'd be able to have more control over situations where socialization with other children occurred (i.e., gatherings with other homeschoolers, sports, Sunday school, social events).

The third, and perhaps most important reason for us to homeschool, was because biblical principles would not be taught in the classroom. As Christians, this was a concern. We'd foster biblical principles at home, but it would've been beneficial to have a well-rounded system that included this.

Sending them to an expensive private Christian school also wasn't an option. Not only because of financial and geographic reasons, but because of my earlier point that this would deny our family the joy of time together. We didn't want to send our children away every day, especially at such a young age.

I owned and ran a full-service beauty salon until Eden's birth. While I knew I wanted to be home to raise our children, I wasn't sure what my role as mother would be other than what I'd seen from friends and parents before me.

I'd volunteer at school, help the kids with their homework, take them to ballet, soccer, and hockey practice, and read them bedtime stories. These were commendable pursuits, yet would this be enough for me?

John told me to think about the homeschooling idea and even suggested I sit down and write a list of pros and cons. A simple enough proposition. Reasons why I should homeschool versus reasons why not. (I highly recommend doing this.)

I gave a contemplative nod, as in *I could do that much*. And I did. I was a parent like you, and I didn't want to fail our children. Therefore, I could at least look at all the options.

I read articles on everything I could get my hands on, from how-to theories to newspaper pieces to documents from the academic world. I noted that prestigious universities sought homeschooled kids for their programs because children educated at home were proven to be self-motivated, eager learners.

I found collective data that stated homeschoolers were proficient at life skills such as cooking and cleaning, that they thought independently and had strong family relationships that continued into adulthood. I attended homeschooling conferences, gleaned resources and materials, and got a feel for what others did.

I took my time and did a lot of soul-searching, asking myself if I had what it took to educate our children. I knew I had the discipline that was needed, the creativity and imagination to make learning fun, and a deep love and passion to be with our kids. It all went on the list.

By the time I'd completed that list, the "pro" side was so long—reasons why I *should* homeschool—that the answer was abundantly clear. In addition, the short "con" side was made up of points that swayed me *toward* homeschooling instead of away from it.

Socialization, for one, is something we already knew that homeschoolers were supposedly lacking. For us, our kids would not lack social skills because they would learn what the real world was like and interact with those around them, regardless of age, sex, or social standing.

Added to this, they'd see how I planned my day, how I accomplished tasks, how I networked with others. They'd learn valuable morals and wouldn't be forced into social settings that were unhealthy or developmentally unsound. In sum, I was positive our children would have the best education at home.

Eden: For me, homeschooling never felt like anything out of the ordinary. In fact, I never gave it much thought that I was homeschooled because all the friends I had growing up knew I was taught at home.

At university, I met peers who were curious about my experience because they didn't know I was homeschooled all the way up to high school. When they realized what my pre-university education entailed, they wanted to know how much credit I gave homeschooling for my good grades, critical-thinking skills, and work ethic.

While university shaped my adult academic years, I attribute a great number of the successes I had in my studies to homeschooling. Being taught at home by my mom never lost its appeal, even as I matured. I grew up loving to learn, read, and discover. Much of the subject matter and how it was relayed is something I've retained and still value to this day.

It's true, I didn't homeschool through a forced crisis or because we had a child with special needs. I homeschooled because I wanted to be with our children and enjoy them in those growing-up years, to help shape them into well-adjusted, healthy, caring, intellectual adults, and to provide a positive influence.

You may have other valid reasons why you're considering homeschooling. Wonderful! Whatever the rationale, we all have our children's best interests at heart.

Let's continue and take a stroll through our day.

WHAT OUR DAY-TO-DAY LOOKED LIKE

We're always learning. Every day of our lives. Yet how many times had I heard kids groan that they hated school. I didn't want our children to feel the same way, so I was going to do my best to ensure that they loved learning.

The secret of homeschooling is to challenge our kids appropriately and to help them find meaning in what they learn. This was my goal, with the added objective of making it fun.

As mentioned earlier, I'd started laying the groundwork when our kids were toddlers. Our days were filled with everything from crafts to interactive activities, to quiet playtime and outdoor fun, to learning cause and effect and how things worked.

Once they reached school age, we added more structure, creating a basic educational routine. That's not to say we didn't veer from it or change things up, because we did.

That's the beauty of homeschooling—the freedom to alter your day, try something you thought impossible another day, or drop everything and have a playday. Sometimes those are needed. It's a fantastic feeling to know you can recharge and not be glued to a set-in-stone schedule *and* not feel guilty over it.

To demonstrate my point on changing things up: When our kids were five and seven, I had what I thought was a splendid idea on how to start our day that would include my husband. After all, he was missing our regular pursuits, and this new idea would be a small compensation. John is usually out the door by 7 a.m. to head to school, so I thought we'd make time for a family morning walk before we all started our day.

It was dark out when I woke the kids. And I can say they were less than thrilled. Had Mommy gone off the deep end with this homeschooling stuff? But as a morning walker myself, and as someone who loved the refreshed feeling that I started with each day, I thought I'd encourage them to see this as a morning adventure. What animals might be out at this hour? What noises would we hear?

Since we live on Lake Huron in beautiful cottage country, it wasn't out of the ordinary to see a fox prance by or witness a herd of deer leap out of the bush or spot an owl on a tall branch. I let the kids decide if they wanted to walk or ride their bikes. We tried different things.

It's true anyone could do the same with their children before their school day, but we didn't have the time constraints that school kids have. There were no lunches to pack, buses to catch, or last-minute projects to stuff into knapsacks. And I wasn't working outside the home, so I didn't need to rush to get myself ready either.

Some mornings, if John had to leave earlier than usual, we walked without him. Again, it was our day to plan as we wished.

While this idea was wonderful in theory, that late-fall adventure only lasted about three weeks. Our children loved outdoor activity, and they were raring to go by eight o'clock once we returned home and had breakfast. But getting up with the birds wasn't the exhilarating adventure I'd hoped for.

When my dear husband empathized with the kids' early-morning grumblings, I decided this brainwave wasn't worth the effort. You can imagine the relief when I suggested we save the physical endeavors to later in the morning or day.

As with everything about homeschooling, we learned as we went, discovering what activities and schedules suited our family. If one thing didn't fit, we tried something else.

After getting our feet wet and gaining a feel for homeschooling, I created a basic schedule that met our needs. It may even work for you.

On the other hand, if your eyes glaze over because you feel our days look *too* structured—no problem. Use your own vision and select concepts that *do* speak to you. Heck, maybe morning walks please your family, or perhaps an early-hour trip to the park.

You may even find particular subjects join together well, like our Art and Storytime as described in the coming pages. Other parts of our daily calendar, you may wish to work at longer or cut completely. You decide when to space snack time, when to end your day.

Early on, I worried about what I might miss that I should be including in our children's education. I can assure you that that feeling passed. I soon realized, as they grew and grasped material, that whatever I might've overlooked, they would learn in good time, just by being part of and experiencing life.

Even the school system doesn't cover every curriculum expectation. Recognizing this fact was a huge *aha!* moment for me, and I can't express the weight this lifted off my shoulders.

My husband the teacher also helped ease my worry. After I started homeschooling and John saw how much we *had* accomplished in a day, he even suggested we finish at noon. His point was that our children were learning a great deal, and without the usual school interruptions and distractions. We didn't need to draw out the day until 3:00.

He was 100 percent right, and there are indeed homeschoolers who call it quits by noon. If there had been struggles, inability to focus, or lack of interest in a certain topic, we could've altered our calendar. But the schedule I arranged was ideal for us, and our kids were soaking it all up.

Unless we planned a day at the museum or library, or another type of field trip, or just a playday with other homeschoolers, we spent the day in class, so to speak. Even on days where I did make other plans, I'd usually book those outings and engagements for the afternoon so we could accomplish our core subjects in the morning.

Eden: The one-on-one attention was a huge benefit of homeschooling because it allowed me to work at my own pace. I could get help on a concept I didn't understand until I mastered it, and time wasn't wasted on lessons I grasped quickly. So much ground was covered this way, and when I arrived at high school, I felt ahead of the game in many subjects.

At university, I attended lectures that a professor slowed down in order to reiterate a theory for the benefit of only a handful of students. Looking around the auditorium, I'd see other students on their phones and talking amongst themselves while waiting for the lesson to continue.

When I look back, I see how beneficial it was that my mom only had to split her attention between two children, not thirty or two hundred and thirty.

I'd also like to talk about learning style: visual, auditory, and kinesthetic. In other words, learning through images and graphs, versus absorbing spoken information, versus understanding through physical movement and touch. It's different for everyone and is key to how one comprehends material. Homeschooling is a conducive environment for tailoring lesson plans that best suit a student's learning needs.

My mom would incorporate modules and activities that allowed my younger brother and me to explore our preferred ways of acquiring information. Unlike a traditional teacher, she witnessed our developmental stages from infancy to adolescence. Therefore, she knew how to rework a lesson in a way that made the content more comprehensible to each of us.

I learn easily by reading instructions. I then make notes and charts in assorted colors to highlight main points. Hart also learns easily by reading, but he grasps ideas kinesthetically because he loves working with his hands.

An example of this was during our biology unit on living organisms when we incorporated all learning styles into one lesson. First, we read and looked at images of cells, then our mom explained what we saw on the page.

Finally, we made replica cells out of Jell-O. A gumdrop represented the nucleus, a jelly bean became the mitochondria, and gummy worms symbolized the Golgi apparatus.

Autonomous or self-directed learning was another valuable tool that I was equipped with through homeschooling. A number of textbooks I worked from included a description of the unit, followed by examples, and then practice questions.

As I grew older, I could work through these lessons alone, with my mom still nearby to answer questions. This method of teaching myself built basic research techniques and fostered transferable skills such as self-discipline.

At this point, you might be wondering what type of curriculum we used. In truth, I wasn't set on any special program. I'd walk the aisles in the homeschooling store in our area, perusing oodles of curricula. Depending on grade level and keeping loosely to what students were learning in school, I picked material per subject as I saw fit.

Sometimes a specific company presented material in one field in a delightful way, yet it waned in another. Some textbooks were kid-friendly with more pictures and less writing. Others provided more hands-on modules with complementary workbooks. Still others were proficient at reviewing key concepts. It was a cornucopia of material that we loved and that excited us—me especially as I wanted to be enthused as I taught.

I should add here that while children can learn through TV, movies, apps, and the internet, our kids didn't habitually sit in front of a screen (including handheld devices). Instead, I encouraged them to discover the world around them in a multitude of ways.

There are, of course, exceptions to using devices regularly. Children with learning disabilities rely on programs available on handheld devices. Parents who work while homeschooling may depend on education from a screen. But as we didn't fall in these areas, I preferred our kids' education to be more hands-on.

That's not to say we didn't watch a children's program or a Disney movie once in a while. But those were often for a treat, or for the odd time when we needed a break, or for the occasional rainy day where it was much more fun to cuddle up on the couch and laugh at Cruella de Vil tracking down spotted pups in her classic red car, honking the horn, and slamming the brakes with her bony foot.

Eden: As much as I love reading, certain topics were enhanced when they were delivered on a screen. After learning about, for example, the War of 1812 in the textbook, it was stimulating to watch re-enactment videos and documentaries.

Planet Earth is another intriguing series that instilled wonder and awe for the natural world and living organisms. These different mediums complemented each other and made lessons more tangible when we could watch footage about what we'd read.

Other times I sat in front of the computer concentrated on interactive math games and French vocabulary voice recordings. Some of these included activities for multiple participants, and when that was the case, Hart would join me. If something was difficult for him to grasp, this gave me the opportunity to guide him instead of asking our mom for help.

For additional curriculum ideas, I liked the notion of somewhat adhering to what kids were learning in school. To that end, the Ministry of Education provided an outline on what was taught at each grade level, something you could also look into with your local or state school board.

It was a splendid resource, allowing me to feature many of the same units at home. Our kids could then share and discuss what they were learning with friends at traditional schools.

For example, in grade 4 when students Eden's age studied a unit on Medieval Times, I taught my own unit. We created castles and moats, combining history, art, and math skills. This was a valuable way to incorporate multiple subjects in a single unit.

Despite Hart being two years younger, he eagerly paid attention. If his sister made a castle, you could bet he wanted to create one, too.

We also visited Medieval Times in Toronto, spent the day at a Middle Ages fest, learned about serfs and the feudal system, and played games depicting life for the rich and poor.

The important thing to remember is we weren't tied to a particular curriculum. Nor do you need to be. You may not even like teaching from a book. It's a learning experience in itself to experiment with what works and what doesn't. Having this freedom is another advantage to homeschooling.

***

Let's move on to what an actual day of homeschooling looked like. For us, homeschool began each morning at 8:30 after breakfast and devotionals. We'd brush our teeth and settle into our daily routine—seven sessions, roughly 40 minutes each.

MATH

Almost always, we began our school day with math. It took many shapes and forms. Some days, when Eden and Hart were learning how to count money, we'd play store. We had a life-sized toy cash register, fake credit cards, and play money. After I'd price a bunch of items throughout the cupboards and set them in different areas of the "store," my two eager students would take turns playing either the clerk or the customer.

We spent many hours filling our carts, Eden and Hart cracking up when I'd play the gum-snapping cashier.

"*Hank!*" I'd shout through chomps of gum to an imaginary employee. "We need a price check in aisle five."

The first time I did this, the kids looked over their shoulders for Hank. When Hank didn't materialize, I tapped my pretend mic. "Where's Hank from Cleaning Products? We need a price check."

Sometimes we'd have to take a break from shopping because we'd be rolling in *our* aisles with bouts of laughter.

This is just one example of how entertaining your days can be, simply by using your imagination. If we weren't playing store, or learning to tell time on a sponge pop-out-hands-and-numbers clock, I'd set up my son with his assignment first, since he was younger.

Sometimes Hart would start with a math workbook, and other times the assignment would be tactile. Stimulating thinking games, for instance, were excellent because they required matching pictures to numbers or rolling dice to record probability.

I'd then review what Eden needed to accomplish. I'd be there to help while they each worked. If no help was needed, I'd re-examine my English/grammar notes, prepping for the next subject.

If you weren't a math genius growing up, believe me when I say I understand your pain. Teaching math to the very young is different from explaining exponents to children approaching high school. However, I found enough simplified math textbooks for older kids and free worksheets online that made lessons easier to grasp.

So take heart if you feel teaching math will be too much of a challenge. There are loads of resources. Be sure to find material that is straightforward and speaks to you. Not only will your confidence be boosted, but you'll have an easier time relaying theories to your children.

ENGLISH/GRAMMAR & PIANO LESSONS

English and grammar studies ranged from reading full-length books to short stories to comic books to textbook narratives. I followed up, quizzing on comprehension—whether orally or on paper.

Spelling and other grammar basics often came in the form of games or puzzles or something homemade that I could dream up. Other times it was pencil to the paper.

I read in massive amounts to our children from the time they were babes, so by school age, they had a good grasp of the English language and would pick up books on their own to fit their interest.

If you also read to your children, don't stop. Children who read more tend to become better learners. Essentially, the more they read, the more they understand. The more they understand, the more they learn.

This was an important feature of homeschooling because our children learned early to read instructions, and, as Eden already pointed out, they could then implement what they'd learned for themselves.

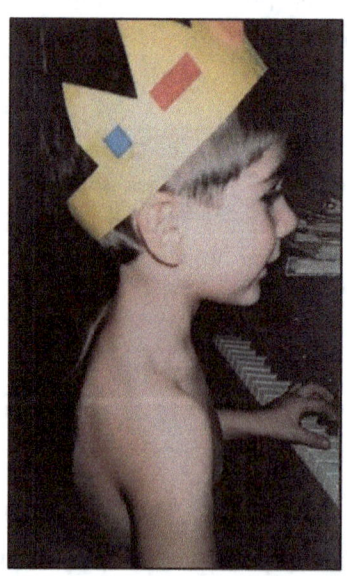

Splitting English/grammar with piano was a refreshing way to break up the morning from the kids working side by side. As I have my grade 8 in piano, a qualification recognizing the highest level of piano expertise, I had a solid understanding in music and the proper technical skills to give our kids a musical background. Add the years I taught piano before having children, and I was eager to pass on my knowledge.

While Eden studied English/grammar, I'd sit with Hart at the piano. After twenty-five minutes or so, we'd switch, and Hart would work on his English/grammar while Eden had her piano lessons.

Passing on a personal skill or talent like this is wholly encouraged. Do you play the guitar and engage your kids in silly musical sessions? Or perhaps you have a background in dance, and your toddlers leap around the house with you to a popular song. We invented our own sweeping routines to ABBA and danced till we flopped. It wasn't the standard Juilliard School type of dance, but did we have a riot!

Maybe your background isn't musical. That's perfectly fine. Whatever the talent—art, archery, writing, baking, juggling, carpentry, public speaking—this is a treasured gift and an opportunity to impart a unique skill to your children.

SNACK & PLAY BREAK

Our 15-minute break usually fell around 10:15 a.m. A few jumping jacks or a change of scenery, such as playing outside, would perk up the kids. Often, they'd munch on their snack outdoors while I set up the next subject. A little fresh air, nourishment, and change of pace rejuvenated them and had them eager to resume class.

FRENCH

This area was a perfect example of how we scouted out unique curriculum to suit our needs. I wasn't thrilled with anything I'd seen for French studies at the homeschooling store. So I looked elsewhere, including online, and ended up finding colorful, illustrated workbooks that we loved from a department store. (Yard sales and consignment shops are also marvelous for unearthing material. We discovered globes, puzzles, science sets, books, and other items we could utilize in projects.)

These vivid French workbooks provided engaging learning for every age and taught the basics—perfect for teachers tackling a language new even to them. Because I enjoyed French in high school and had a partial French-speaking background, I managed to follow along easily.

To break up the bookwork, we sang and danced to French children's songs that we'd listen to regularly. Whether playing French or Spanish or Mandarin tunes, this is a terrific way to introduce languages to your children.

For something else invigorating, we'd create a French menu—later even cooking the meal. We used our senses to describe how things around the house smelled or felt.

We trekked outside and learned words like *cat*,

car, *lake*. Then we'd phrase a sentence. The sillier the better. The cat is eating the car and jumping in the lake. *Le chat mange la voiture et saute dans le lac.*

It seemed the foreign-language equivalent to the early *Dick and Jane* books. But for young children, it was important to foster a zest for learning another tongue. And learning in any capacity was a major building block.

You can imagine how quickly 30-40 minutes of a new language flew by when leaving regular deskwork to investigate elsewhere. Furthermore, who knew when a simple word or action would come into play?

When Eden and Hart were older, we often spent the whole morning speaking in French, only falling back on English when necessary. As with music, this is another example of an opportunity to teach or pass on your own skills to your children.

Do you have an Italian background? German? Did you once study sign language? Why not share this? Any second language will benefit your children as they mature and explore this big world.

Eden: Along with the French activities above, we also applied our growing language skills by writing letters to friends and family who live in France, using a French-English dictionary to translate words we didn't know. By applying French lessons to a real-life situation, we gained confidence in sending cards to people we knew.

However, French was the subject I was most nervous about when I started high school. I worried that I wouldn't have the proper pronunciation or that I'd have too limited a vocabulary to express myself.

It turned out I knew grammatical concepts and conjugation rules that my peers had not yet learned. With the encouragement of my teacher, I even went on a three-month exchange to France. My exchange partner is one of my best friends to this day.

Languages may be an intimidating subject to teach. Just as Eden went on to study French in university, this could be true for your children with other subjects translating into a career or future studies in unexpected ways, too.

ART & STORYTIME

Eden: This was probably my favorite part of our day. My mom would provide an art exercise for us to carry out, and while Hart and I crafted, she'd sit in the rocking chair nearby and read three or four chapters from a novel.

Some of our projects were extensive. Others, simple. We drew, practiced cursive, made collages with leaves that we'd gathered, created butterflies by painting coffee filters with watercolors, shredded images from magazines and fabricated accordion-type pictures.

Some tasks took several weeks to complete, such as sewing pillows from fabrics we'd each selected. Others combined science and math as in our shoebox pulley system of Jack climbing the beanstalk.

Other projects coincided with Mother's Day or birthdays. T-shirts that Hart and I designed still hang in my mom's closet.

The novels, which we loved hearing our mom read, were linked with other themes we were learning about, through their historical setting or geography. Stories that stood out were fictional tales of a boy's life and adventures in Egypt and another about a child's experience during the war.

One such book, *I Am David*, in which a boy escapes from a concentration camp and tries to find his mother, often had my mom in tears. One day, I remember her weeping at a particularly sad point and asking Hart to finish reading the chapter. He willingly obliged.

Working at our art projects didn't seem like an effort because we were so wrapped up in these stories. It was a winning combination that we looked forward to year after year.

LUNCH

Eden: Lunches were also made appealing. Some days we'd eat under a blanket fort. Other days, we'd have a picnic outside or eat in the upper canopy of the swing set.

It was our job to wash and cut veggies that we kept in a big container.

We also learned how to use different kitchen tools to make meals colorful and attractive, even if it was only shaping grilled cheese sandwiches into hearts or forming fruits and veggies into bizarre objects. Occasionally, we'd haul out the marshmallows, gumdrops, pretzels, and chocolate chips and create silly people.

Introducing us to cooking by making it fun was an integral part to sparking interest in the kitchen. This then paved the way when it came to preparing more complicated dishes.

HISTORY & GEOGRAPHY

After lunch, we delved into history, followed by geography. I learned a lot myself through these studies since I had no recollection of being taught certain material in school, such as what the five major peninsulas in Europe were or the fascinating characteristics of the Dead Sea.

One history book had short unit chapters on, for example, ancient Egypt. Amid the text, there were photos of actual pyramids, obelisks, papyrus sheets, and hieroglyphics. As Eden already mentioned, many of the textbooks we used provided questions at the end of a chapter on what was covered in the section. It was a meaningful reinforcement for what the kids had read, and short enough without being boring.

This type of recap was an idea I adopted for

ongoing lessons. Again, we'd combine history and art, utilizing our knowledge to make our own hieroglyphics on papyrus paper.

We did fun activities away from books as well. In geography, we hung a huge world map on the wall. I'd call out a country or capital, and Eden and Hart would run to the map with paper boats glued on Popsicle sticks (created during art one day) and place their boats on the correct location. They learned all the countries of the world this way, as well as other geographical points.

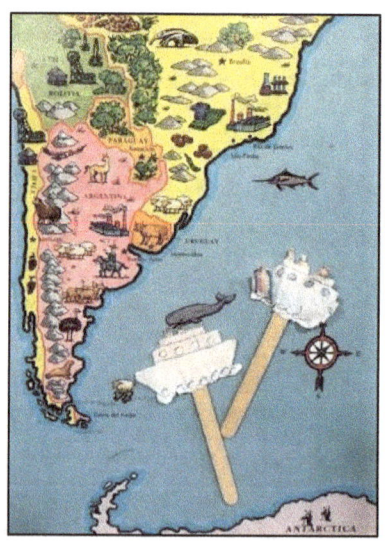

We weren't born in the USA, but our children still learned each state and its capital on a magnetic puzzle board. Sometimes they'd piece together only Midwest states or Northeast states, learning characteristics or points of interest for that part of the country. Effortless things like this kept learning from becoming stagnant.

A MOTHER-DAUGHTER ACCOUNT ON WHY IT WAS A SUCCESS

Through our history lessons, they studied slavery, the Civil War, the great stock market crash, the bombing of Hiroshima, the assassinations of JFK and Martin Luther King, Jr., Watergate, and other major events that impacted the United States and world history.

For Canada's provinces and capitals, I made up a song to the tune of "If You're Happy And You Know It, Clap Your Hands." It started with "British Columbia, Alberta, Saskatchewan..." *clap, clap*. You get it. Easy-peasy. It was juvenile, but our kids were only six and four at the time. They learned the provinces and capitals through this song and can still recite them today.

My son was so young when I taught them the song, his Newfoundland came out as New*found*land. No matter. They knew the country they lived in, east to west, something we could build on as they grew older. And we did.

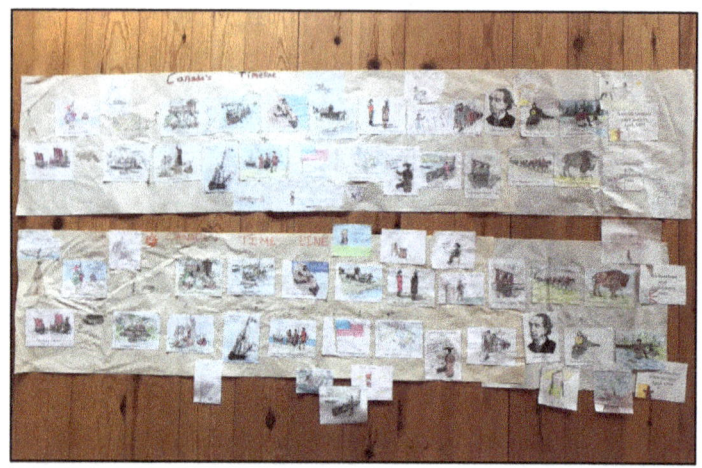

They learned about Canadian Confederation and that our country is a peaceful nation. They studied Canada's vast landscape, how we contributed to both World Wars. They knew early on that Canada was home to hockey.

Later on, we examined politics and how the House of Commons operates—something my son still finds fascinating. We even watched real-world footage of our political leaders in action. This truly brought politics and social studies to life. It also inspired our kids to be conscious of human rights, of their duty to vote once they became of age, and, in general, how to be good global citizens.

SCIENCE

Since science is an understanding of how things work through observation and experimentation, this idea was important to nurture. To be honest, I had never been a huge fan of science, so I needed to be as enthusiastic as possible and make this subject as captivating as I could.

We discussed weather patterns, climates, and seasons. We combined dish soap, glitter, and water to produce a tornado in a bottle. We created paper dials with cloud images, then trucked outside to match them with the day's current cloud formations. In the winter, we turned maple syrup into taffy in the snow. We designed weather charts and made funny props in which to record the weather.

Sure, there were notes to take. But what kid wants to sit and read about tests and trials when they could conduct their own experiments? Plus, when it came to taking notes, we tried to be creative. We'd construct display boards as students did in school and present topics of interest at science fairs and other community events.

Retirement homes, for example, loved when homeschoolers came in and talked about their exhibits. This gave our children the chance to mingle and share their knowledge with others in the community. Again, we combined art with science when the opportunity arose.

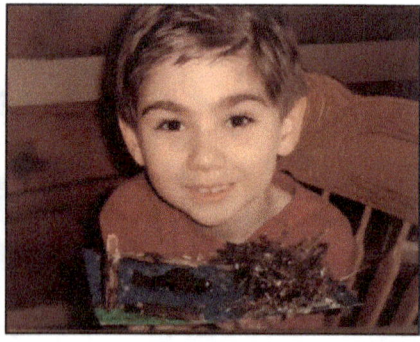

We did practical experiments by using basic things around the house. Spools of thread, food coloring, string, baking soda, vinegar. We made batteries, dyed celery stalks, produced crystals, built Jell-O cells. When we learned about photosynthesis, we grew plants. We cooked. We baked. On occasion, we asked the butcher for cows' hearts or other organs, and we'd dissect them.

Once again, we learned what children in school were studying at the same grade level. When they explored bridges and structures, we dove into that as well and created our own replicas.

There is so much information online and suggestions for easy experiments, you could do science all day if that appeals to you! It doesn't need to be difficult. Whether through books or by firsthand investigation, we kept it simple, learning concepts that intrigued and excited us.

So take heart and don't fret over what you're *not* teaching your kids. When I recalled the angst I once felt about not providing a complete education for our children, I have to shake my head at the absurdity of it. There is no doubt that our kids were learning!

PHYS ED

Eden: As some science experiments took time to develop, it made sense to swap science investigations periodically for other things. It worked out that every other day, we'd switch science for phys ed.

One activity that we loved was the obstacle course our mom set up outside. Starting at the playset, we'd have to scale the rock wall, swing hand-to-hand from the monkey bars, climb the ladder, descend the cargo net, and go up and down the slide five times.

Then we'd run around the house twice, do five somersaults, jump ten times through a skip rope, and kick a ball around pylons. The possibilities were endless, and the options were straightforward enough to vary the order/amount of each task another time. Mom would clock us and cheer us on.

We also had a basketball net and hockey nets for road hockey. There was plenty of equipment in the garage, from skateboards and hula hoops to lacrosse sticks and baseball gear. Sometimes we'd have other homeschoolers over and organize more structured games.

We were also involved in team sports like soccer and hockey, as well as other athletics such as tennis and swimming lessons. So we had lots of physical activity along with the camaraderie that developed from team sports.

As long as your children are active, a formal gym class isn't necessary. I can tell you from watching our kids dash around all day during school and then play outside after we finished our work, they received a healthy dose of daily exercise.

***

Now that you've caught a glimpse of what our day-to-day looked like, it's a good time to sit back and take a deep breath. If you're reading this book in one sitting—which is easy to do—you might feel a bit overwhelmed at all the information, the schedule, and the pursuits. Trust me, nothing came together overnight. It took a bit of trial and error and time to develop.

Remember, this structure worked for *us*. You might discover a similar pattern works for you. Or you may feel you don't want any structure. One day, math at 9:00 a.m., and the next day at 2:30 p.m. Or no math at all for two days. That's the benefit of homeschooling. You decide what fits your family. If you detest schedules, find your own model for teaching.

It's also important to note that regardless of best intentions, things didn't always come together as planned. If we ran late into another subject because a project was taking longer than expected or because something else came up and we got off track, we wouldn't fret. There was always the next day to resume our regular schedule if we chose.

There are dozens of other reasons why things won't go according to plan when you homeschool. Flared tempers. Sick children. Unexpected blows. But that's life. You'll learn to roll with the punches.

Sure, you'll get discouraged. But when you think back to why you chose to homeschool—ultimately because you want the best for your children—those frustrating emotions will fade away, and you'll bounce back the next day, or the day after, ready to start fresh.

At the end of this chapter, you will find a chart to help you visualize what our structured days looked like.

***

The last thing I'd like to cover in this section wasn't so much part of our day-to-day as it was part of our year-to-year. Near the end of our annual homeschooling term, John and the kids would surprise me with a "Teacher Appreciation" cake for my dedication and perseverance. It was a touching gesture that truly made me feel loved and valued.

As the cake-giving became a regular yearly event, it shouldn't have come as a surprise. But it always did. Homeschooling has its ups and downs, and as I'd look at this beautiful cake and reflect on the energy I'd put into educating our kids each year, the floodgates would open and the moment was commonly met with tears of joy.

I treasured our modest little teaching world and was even more grateful for the devoted husband I had. Through John's adoring initiative with the cake—one of many—our children saw and appreciated what a supportive and loving father he was, and how much our family meant to him.

A Mother-Daughter Account On Why It Was A Success

I don't know what situation you're in, or if anyone upholds and encourages you. But my hope is that you have a special someone to walk this homeschooling journey with, whether it's a spouse, a parent, or a close friend. That reassurance is a rare gift and something to be cherished.

HOMESCHOOLING

TIME	MONDAY	TUESDAY	WEDNESDAY	THURSDAY	FRIDAY
8:30-9:15	Math	Math	Math	Math	Math
9:20-10:10	English/Piano	English/Piano	English/Piano	English/Piano	English/Piano
10:15-10:30	SNACK	TIME	AND	PLAY	BREAK
10:35-11:20	French	French	French	French	French
11:25-12:10	Art/Storytime	Art/Storytime	Art/Storytime	Art/Storytime	Art/Storytime
12:15-12:45	L	U	N	C	H
12:50-1:30	History	History	History	History	History
1:35-2:15	Geography	Geography	Geography	Geography	Geography
2:20-3:00	Science	PhysEd	Science	PhysEd	Science

SPECIAL DAYS

The last chapter covered our structured days, displayed our class timeline, and, I hope, formed thoughts on how schedules and lessons might work for you. Here, I want to share a collection of amusing and, at times, unique stuff that we did apart from the normal school day.

As I mentioned earlier, we live in beautiful cottage country on Lake Huron. We took great advantage of that. Some days that were too nice to work inside, we'd spread a blanket on the lawn and study outside. Other days, we'd pack our books, take a lunch, and ride our bikes to the lighthouse where we'd complete our lessons under the tall white structure, with the beach in the background.

Maybe you have a similar or unique setting that would freshen or change the pace. Do you live on a farm? Maybe a day of hanging out with the horses or studying in the barn on bales of hay would tickle your kids' fancy. What about taking advantage of a camp setting? Pitch a tent in your backyard. Study around a campfire. Let those creative juices flow and make use of your surroundings.

For us, after a few hours of studying by the lighthouse, we'd dip our feet in the water, play on the jungle set, and search for rare-shaped stones in the sand. This was another opportunity to learn, scout, focus. Perhaps your kids would love the chance to gather unusual shells or beach glass. We collected heart-shaped stones since our son is named Hart.

Following our day of leisurely learning, we'd bike back home in time to prepare supper.

The great outdoors was a holistic classroom, and the kids even made good use of the forest right outside our door. They'd haul out their dad's tools to construct tree forts, rope swings, and rafts, later proudly showing off their structures when their dad came home from work.

Winter days were just as energizing, often balancing learning with play. We'd take an afternoon off and drink hot chocolate while building a fort. We'd snowshoe or cross-country ski. Or just build a snowman if the weather conditions were right.

One time, John and his little helpers even built an ice rink so we had the option to head into the backyard to skate if poor weather conditions didn't allow us to drive into town.

A Mother-Daughter Account On Why It Was A Success

Eden: We also looked forward to every other Friday morning. We joined a homeschooling group where we met in a church basement and formed small classes with seven or eight children in each. Every parent who brought their kids shared their knowledge or expertise in key areas and headed a unique class.

One mom had her black belt in karate and coached us in the art of self-defense. A bilingual mom taught French. Another walked us through cooking special dishes. One parent who was a chemistry buff taught science. Another showed kids how to embroider. My mom taught music and dance. After lunch and a bit of playtime in the gym, we'd wrap up and go our separate ways until the next time.

Our bi-weekly gatherings with other homeschoolers were invigorating, busy, and loads of fun. Between swimming lessons, library events, sports practices, youth groups, and our own outings and field trips, they added just the right amount of interaction.

HOMESCHOOLING

If you choose to homeschool your children, do yourself a favor and seek out other homeschoolers or groups that resonate with your beliefs. It's a wonderful opportunity to make friends—adults and children alike—and share stories, challenges, and successes. Being with like minds also helped me realize I wasn't alone in this endeavor.

Because it was important to introduce the idea of serving to our children, we routinely found ways to help others. One time, we helped a gentleman paint his place. Another time, when we still lived in the city, we made cookies and had a lemonade stand.

While we baked and prepared our stand, I suggested we give the money made to charity. The kids were happy to do this. For them, the fun was in baking, sampling our goods, and playing mini salesmen at the side of the road. That was okay. The idea was to instill an attitude of giving, and we made this part of our homeschooling practice.

Another activity that gave us a break from daily routine was playing the piano at retirement homes. Since I volunteered monthly, once Eden and Hart were old enough to carry a tune on the piano, they regularly joined me and played their own selections for the seniors.

Needless to say, the residents adored seeing the children and listening to them tickle the ivories. Of course, being so young, our kids were a bit intimidated by these old folks fawning over them. But the atmosphere was friendly and tender, and my little performers developed polite, sincere attitudes toward their audience.

Eden and Hart grew to understand the importance of showing compassion for others and learned how to relate to people outside of their age group. Along with playing the piano in front of an audience, this built their self-confidence.

We also headed to the library each week and returned home with two huge cloth bags full of picture books. Reading and enjoying the books in a variety of ways was a regular highlight. We'd draw pictures or create real-life settings of treasured scenes.

We'd memorize favorite lines or silly passages and make images of quirky characters or things that delighted us.

A Mother-Daughter Account On Why It Was A Success

Simply by bringing books to life and thinking outside the box, our children learned how to take an idea and expand on it. In a rich way that developed intrinsically, they could pinpoint key factors in stories and understand vital content.

Picture books evolved into novels, and by the time our daughter was in grade 8, her comprehension skills were so acute, she was even able to teach herself more advanced math. I was there to guide her, but she didn't need my help.

Additional outings we relished were field trips, sometimes with other homeschoolers, sometimes on our own. We went to rural playhouses. We took hikes and nature walks. We traveled to a pioneer village, scenic caves, science centers, museums, zoos, maple syrup farms, even mines.

Some days, we'd forgo piano lessons and pull out all the merrymaking instruments from our bin. We'd march around the house, playing recorders, harmonicas, melodicas. We'd pound the drums, shake the maracas, flutter the tambourine. Anything to make music. We tried different sounds and unique combinations. We played whatever felt right. It was unorganized, a cacophony of noise, and it was a blast.

Sometimes we'd invite other homeschoolers to our house. One Valentine's Day, the children all made heart-themed crafts. Another time, we baked an ethnic dessert from my heritage. For birthdays, we'd welcome a dozen kids to help celebrate Eden's or Hart's special day.

When the holidays approached, the three of us would bake Christmas cookies, wrap them up in festive containers, and set them out for the garbage man, an elderly neighbor, someone in need, or anyone whom our kids thought might be blessed by such a surprise.

As with everything, what Eden and Hart were learning was put to good use. More significantly, they began to grasp the wisdom of including acts of kindness in their day.

On occasion, we'd hit the books in the morning and shop in the afternoon. The kids would take their chore money and buy a treat for themselves. They'd perform the whole transaction without help from me or the cashier—who would smile at me in the background as they carefully counted their coins.

Those days of playing store gave our children confidence in handling money and dealing with people in the consumer world, and their beaming faces showed they were proud of their accomplishment.

A Mother-Daughter Account On Why It Was A Success

Eden: From the time Hart and I were young, our parents fostered a love for the arts. Every year, they planned a family weekend away in Stratford, home to the annual Shakespeare Festival and theater. We'd walk the streets of this unique cultural town and take in musicals and plays like *The Three Musketeers*, *A Midsummer Night's Dream*, *Oliver Twist*, *The Music Man*, and *The Comedy of Errors*.

My enjoyment of these plays came from the language, the plot, and the symbolic elements, which no doubt influenced my decision to major in English and take as many Shakespeare courses as possible.

Hart, who is double majoring in French and Legal Studies, and who took pleasure in clowning around as a child, reveled in the dramatics, the costumes, and the music.

To this day, our Stratford family weekend is a yearly event. Hart and I will even book our own tickets and go together to see a production of *Hamlet* or *Macbeth*.

Of course, even non-homeschoolers can partake in outings like these. But we had the flexibility to take excursions as often as we wished. Moreover, I saw opportunity to learn in everything we did, and it was humbly gratifying to witness our children grow in understanding and appreciation through these expeditions.

There were also tender occasions where we'd rescue a hurt animal and nurture it back to health. One time, on our way home from the library, we witnessed a neighborhood cat mauling a chipmunk. I stopped the car, ran out, and shooed the cat away, and we brought the hurt chipmunk home.

We borrowed a friend's small cage and nursed the chipmunk back to health, letting it go once it was strong enough. We did the same for injured birds and once for a baby rabbit that had wounded its leg.

The love and diligence our kids displayed, springing out of bed in the mornings to feed and look after these helpless creatures, was heartwarming and yet another example of learning the lesson of compassion through real-world acts. As well, it brought zoology, the study of animals, to life. It was a plus Eden and Hart didn't have to rush off to school and wait all day until they could come home to check on their patient.

They proved they were responsible and trustworthy—good preparation for having their own pet. We later adopted a kitten from the Humane Society. With devotion and attentiveness, they took turns feeding and brushing their new housemate and cleaning its litter. These ongoing tasks increased their love and respect for all creatures.

Other fun activities came in the form of special occasions. Some of you might know, in my professional life, I write a bestselling mystery series. I'm not sure if my passion for solving riddles and plotting these mysteries had any influence on Eden and Hart, but they loved detective work, like finding clues to solve problems and decipher puzzles.

Eden: I remember waking up on Valentine's Day once, when my mom had chocolate hearts with hidden messages attached to ribbons dangling from the ceiling. And birthdays weren't just opening presents and blowing out candles on a cake. She'd fabricate riddles and rhymes and construct obstacles or trails in order for us to locate our gifts.

A birthday cake might even have something special baked inside. This would greet us first thing in the morning, and we'd celebrate, taking a break from typical learning that day.

These are things everyone celebrates, but with our mom, we never knew what to expect next. She poured everything into enlightening us, and it was exciting how she created fascinating and unique ways for us to celebrate special days.

Playtime, after our school day ended, was another creative part of our day. We'd meet with other homeschoolers and play in our clubhouse or hike to the creek that we called the Clay Club. We'd slosh around in the creek and later bring home buckets of clay and make sculptures.

As Eden and Hart became older, their interests and desire to learn broadened. One year, they wanted to plant a garden outside. My husband helped them prepare the soil, and I guided them with a few tips, but they tackled most of the gardening on their own, planting, watering, and weeding faithfully, later enjoying carrots, onions, squash, and tomatoes.

The carrots were a tad misshaped, and the squash didn't grow as large as the picture on the packet indicated, but we still looked at the garden as a big success.

A MOTHER-DAUGHTER ACCOUNT ON WHY IT WAS A SUCCESS

Special days also meant the kids could spend an afternoon doing whatever they liked. Eden taught herself how to play drums and the guitar. Hart picked up the sax and violin. Eden would read the classics like Hemingway and Fitzgerald for pleasure. Hart would make big fat pretzels, homemade pasta, or oodles of French pastries called *macarons*.

Perhaps I can't chalk everything up to homeschooling, but intrinsic learning was at the core of the things they did and enjoyed.

These weren't the popular activities other kids their age were doing. It wasn't spending hours on social media or computer games, and it wasn't hanging out at the mall. Yet it was pleasing that Eden and Hart had other productive goals. More so, it was rewarding that they never felt they were missing out.

After reading these pages, you probably have a

good grasp of the types of things we did separate from the books. My hope is that in sharing some of our experiences, you'll feel inspired and ready to put your own skill set to use. The ideas are truly limitless as to what you and your kids can do!

HURDLES AND CRITICISMS

As with everything that is of importance or worth the effort, homeschooling comes with hurdles and criticisms. One of the first hurdles we faced was disapproval from particular family members, questioning if we were making the best choice for our children.

My father, specifically, found homeschooling difficult to accept because it was unfamiliar to him. This was discouraging. Having parental support meant a great deal, but we couldn't live our lives waiting for that to happen, especially when we knew this was the right thing for us.

I could save this hurdle for the Blessings section, but it's pertinent here. While I initially beat myself up over the lack of support, a beautiful thing happened. In time, my father saw how his grandchildren were not only learning from our unconventional method of teaching but actually flourishing and succeeding. What's more, he became one of our chief supporters.

He'd mail us newspaper clippings on the benefits of homeschooling, articles from universities that praised homeschoolers, and anything else he could get his hands on regarding this topic. He'd also proudly applaud our kids to his friends and colleagues.

I share this because while you, too, may face family members who are antagonistic about your decision, I encourage you to let time do its thing. I understand if you're thinking, *sure, easier said than done*. But if you know in your heart that homeschooling is what you're destined to do, others will eventually see the wisdom in your decision as your children mature and prosper. It may take a bit of time. But trust me, the transformation you see in others, from firing squad to cheering squad, will provide peace and closure, not to mention validation that you were right in your choice.

Homeschooling also came with sacrifices. In our case, I chose to be a stay-at-home mom while teaching our kids. Because I wasn't working outside the home, that implied a loss of income. Yet, if I'd still had my business, I would've been out the door early and would've needed to pay a tutor or someone to fill in for me to teach our children in those hours I was gone.

This, to me, wasn't ideal. It also didn't feel like homeschooling at its core, as no one loved or cared about educating our children as much as we did.

Furthermore, I knew how tired I'd been after work each day. How would I fit in even half of our activities and events if our schooling had been squeezed in and around Mom's work life? There were only so many hours in a day, and while other parents juggled and balanced a homeschool-why-you-work scenario, for me personally, I needed to be rested each day and fully present.

In today's pandemic world, many parents are indeed managing schedules to fit the challenges of working and educating their children at home. If you've had to put your career on hold temporarily to teach your kids, maybe consider that this is a sacrifice that will yield many rewards and will pay off in the long run. It might even lead you to discover an unexpected new joy.

Speaking of unexpected new joys, this is a good time to expand on my writing life. I'm the author of the Valentine Beaumont comedy mystery series. My gutsy heroine is a beautician and part-time sleuth who has a knack for turning her beauty tools into weapons to catch crooks. Following the release of my second book, I became a *USA Today* bestselling author. But the road to publishing wasn't easy.

When our children were small, I discovered I loved writing. It seemed silly to share this passion with anyone because, in truth, I had very little time to write. However, it was important to keep at it, no matter how slow. I loved homeschooling, but as an individual, it was thrilling to work toward something that fueled me.

Through odd hours here and there, I learned my craft, and once our daughter was in high school, I began winning writing contest after contest. I thought I'd spend one more year homeschooling our son, but my husband said it was time to start thinking of my own goals. I followed his advice.

I officially homeschooled for ten years, more if you count the energy I put into their toddler years. The time was indeed right to follow my dream of being published. By the time my first novel came out, our daughter had just started university.

> **Eden**: You read about the logistics and hurdles my mom shared in this section, but I'd like to highlight the sacrifices a homeschooling parent makes. Homeschooling

was always the norm for me, so growing up, I didn't realize the amount of time and energy my mom dedicated to educating us.

It was up to her to plan and teach well-rounded lessons that went beyond our home classroom. She set aside her own career to focus her attention on homeschooling, to research community events, initiate picnics with other homeschoolers, and decide what subjects to teach.

There were definitely days that must have tested her patience. Not only was she educating us, but she had to deal with our moods, our frustrations if we didn't grasp something, and, at times, our crappy behavior. Somehow, she seemed to handle even the toughest days with patience and grace.

In the end, I reaped from homeschooling all the things my mom poured into it. As an adult, I'm so appreciative that she gave us an amazing education that consisted of field trips and even piano lessons that I dreaded as a child. Now I love sitting and playing the piano, and I find it rewarding learning new music.

Handling outside criticism was an entirely different beast. Despite the number of supporters you have in the decision to homeschool, there will always be those who are diametrically opposed.

Even now, writing a book like this could leave the door open to new criticism and opinions on how we raised our children. Some may feel we were too lax; others may feel we were too stringent.

I've always welcomed the sincere, curious minds when people ask what homeschooling is like or how I had the patience or creativity to teach our own children. Some even graciously admitted they could never homeschool their kids. Others confessed they weren't up to the sacrifices or the thought of losing an income. They were valid concerns.

When it comes to those intrigued but fearful about homeschooling, I often suggested they try it and see what it was like. After all, some didn't give themselves permission to even go there in their mind. For those who say they don't have a creative bone in their body to teach their own child, I pointed out that a bit of ingenuity went a long way.

Haven't we all, at a minimum, used our imagination to get our kids to eat their peas, wash their hands, make their beds? Transfer that cleverness to the classroom.

Dump some buttons or pasta shells on the table, or fun shapes on a felt board, and show your kids how to add and subtract. Hang a chalkboard or whiteboard and let them write down an interesting fact or inspirational quote of the day. Teach them science by experimenting with everyday materials at home.

Truthfully, the more you "do" in homeschooling, the more the imagination flows on how to teach, what tools to use, exciting projects to try. You have more at your fingertips than you realize, and it's an exhilarating feeling to know your children can learn from those easy, straightforward items at your disposal.

Even if parents feel they aren't creative, there are

so many resources from which to collect ideas. Add that to one's dedication to teach their children, and there's no possible way to fail.

Those were my responses for the intrigued. For others, who felt it was their place to set me straight on what was wrong with homeschooling, the mother bear in me came out.

The naysayers didn't know the effort it took to instruct and discipline our children, the strength needed to accomplish goals when homeschooling was clearly not the norm. I told myself there were enough other challenges and to save my energy and not debate my case. But the negative comments I endured were difficult to ignore.

Interestingly, every time someone hassled me, they fired the same questions in the same order. It was disheartening to feel the need to defend our reasons for teaching outside of school, but I wanted people to know how positive an experience it was.

When my answers rendered them silent, I could see the light bulb pop on with their last point, sure they had me with this one. Wasn't I worried about our kids' social interaction? (Like this had never dawned on me.) Some said it with a polite smile. Trying to be helpful. Others with a frown.

At times, it was hard to find grace when others scoffed at me or talked behind my back. I knew I was giving our children a lifelong gift by choosing this path, and I prayed that one day God would bless my efforts. But meanwhile, those moments were crushing.

Though I'd share an upsetting experience with my husband, he didn't see how others treated me or truly understand the hurt I felt as a mom. He was at work every day. No one ever challenged him like they did me. Maybe it was because he was a male, or because he was a paid teacher, and that put him in a different bracket. That was just a guess.

To be supportive, John even suggested that these parents might feel guilty that they hadn't considered homeschooling their own children. Or if they had, they weren't willing to make sacrifices, or extend themselves for their children's sake, or most likely, do something that would break from societal norms. That perhaps they felt threatened by our experiences, by how well-mannered our children were. His thoughts were reasonable and gave me pause to reflect.

By then, I'd become accustomed to being ignored by a handful of mothers in the community because of their obvious disapproval, but the hurt never ceased. One particular mom at hockey every week sent me judgmental looks and made deriding remarks: What could I possibly teach our kids at home? Wasn't I worried our children would fall behind what was being taught at the same grade level at school? Wasn't I afraid of how different our kids would be from others?

Each week, I'd respond to her comments, all the while, asking myself why I was explaining anything to this woman. I mentioned the exciting things we were learning at home—the projects, the inventiveness, the development.

I guaranteed that not only were our kids keeping up with what school kids were learning but that they were surpassing them. How could they not? There were three of us in our little classroom, not 25 to 30. There was no social troubleshooting, no assemblies, no pizza or milk money to collect. And in response to her claim that our children might be different from others, I said with optimism, "I'm counting on it."

This mother was relentless. There was one specific occasion that I will never forget. One night, she sat beside me in the stands as our boys played hockey together, and she blatantly asked the favorite question of all: wasn't I bothered that our kids weren't getting out and socializing?

I'm certain my jaw dropped a foot. We were sitting side by side in the arena, and our boys were playing hockey on the rink with twenty other boys. All I could manage was, "He's *here*, isn't he?"

It was defeating, facing these individuals, but at least our children didn't have those obstacles. In fact, many of their peers were in awe, wishing they, too, could be homeschooled. One of my son's friends thought it'd be cool to eat steak every day at lunch. I didn't know where he got that idea, but a lunch without bologna sandwiches seemed to seal the deal for him.

The remarkable thing about my hockey-mom experience was that several years later, in high school, my daughter tutored this woman's son. I often wondered if she remembered her disparaging words to me. Probably not. But this turn of events brought peace and ultimately closure to my interaction with her.

Eden: The socialization topic is something I'll weigh in on now. For people who don't know all that homeschooling entails, I understand why they're curious about this aspect.

In my family's case, during our homeschooling years, my brother and I were both involved in sports leagues, volunteering, and youth groups that brought us into contact with people of all ages. We were fortunate to have a diverse and well-balanced homeschooling experience.

However, I'm naturally a shyer person and have to push myself out of my comfort zone when meeting new people. Maybe these are attributes people tend to associate with homeschooled kids, but this is simply my personality. Homeschooling didn't dictate it or hinder me from making friends.

My brother, who was homeschooled alongside me, has a personality that is the complete opposite of mine. He's outgoing and makes friends easily. We were both raised in the same setting and are both adequately equipped to handle ourselves in social situations, but we still have different personalities and approach situations differently.

I never felt looked down upon by my new high school classmates when they learned I was homeschooled. Usually they just wanted to know if I got recess when learning at home!

Whatever the reasons one homeschools, whether it's forced because of a world-wide health crisis or because of personal reasons, pack a mentally strong arsenal for people who impose their opinions on you. Homeschooling today may be more accepted and tolerated than it was when I began. But going into it with eyes wide open will be a benefit, and you'll be prepared to speak up if you so choose.

BLESSINGS

Though I stood firm and upheld our reasons when needed for educating our children, I also continued to lean on the loving, fulfilling friendships that I made through homeschooling and my church community.

Little by little, day by day, year by year, we saw the long-term, positive impacts of homeschooling, evidenced by how our children blossomed into courteous young adults with strong morals and a high sense of integrity, without an attitude of entitlement.

Sharing our experience has been extremely humbling, and I suppose this book has been inside me for many years. The truth is, I never once gave myself credit or dwelled on the blessings when I was in the midst of our homeschooling venture.

We accomplished so much in those days, yet there was often a niggling doubt that I might have missed out on parts of our children's education. Had I been thorough enough? Would our kids turn out as I hoped? But recently, a good friend pointed out that our kids' academic successes meant I'd covered my bases. And through hard work, trial and error, a curious mind, and a deep love for my children, I taught myself to be a teacher. That allowed me to give our children the gifts I hoped for when I started our homeschool journey.

So please know that if I could do it, so can you!

***

At first, it was the small things our kids did that made us smile. The automatic *please* and *thank you*—not just to us but to everyone. Making their beds, putting their shoes away when coming in from outside, cleaning up after they played or worked.

Taking time to demonstrate neat habits may sound like simple, good parenting, but this was part of our lifestyle of learning. While I could've concentrated only on studies, I wanted our children to be well-rounded and appreciate that all things needed care. In essence, being respectful of themselves and of the things around them.

> **Eden**: The start of my adult years revealed benefits of homeschooling that went beyond the academic perks. During the thirteen years I spent learning at home, my mom cultivated many invaluable life skills. For instance, I learned how to cook and prepare a well-balanced diet, do laundry and yardwork, manage finances, and organize different areas of my life.
>
> Fast-forward to my university years living alone, and I knew how to take care of household responsibilities and stay healthy all while managing my studies.

A Mother-Daughter Account On Why It Was A Success

It was remarkable to see Eden and Hart mature in every way. They learned how to spend wisely and how to save. How to give and how to receive.

I can clearly see them sitting on the piano bench time and again at the seniors' homes, unsure of this environment yet trusting me for guidance. In a sweet way that developed slowly, their self-esteem and confidence expanded beyond them, and as they grew into adults, I observed firsthand that giving became intrinsic to who they are today.

As they became older, it was touching to hear their hockey coaches thank our kids for the small gift they had bestowed on them at the end of a season for volunteering their time, to witness Eden's and Hart's bosses at their part-time jobs compliment them on their work ethics and polite, helpful manners.

At those moments, memories would flood me of our homeschooling days when Eden and Hart would eagerly bake and wrap cookies for less fortunate people or make gifts for others, or how they took initiative on projects and worked hard with diligence and care.

The compassion in them bloomed in other ways, from those gentle times when they looked after helpless creatures, to defending those in need as young adults.

I knew of instances where our children stood up for someone who was being unfairly treated or bullied. They didn't care that others might mock them. They knew right from wrong, and though they risked becoming unpopular, they weren't going to cower. In fact, they were admired for their integrity.

The blessings continued in the form of awards and scholarships well into university as well as praise from professors. While these things indeed made us proud, what touched us greatly was how their deep-rooted love for learning not only shone through in their studies and academic life but also resulted in a respect for the wider world.

The most humbling blessings have come from our children's love and gratitude to us. Helpful acts of service when they're home visiting, such as weeding the garden or piling wood. Thoughtful, handmade cards from university declaring how much they appreciated the hard work and dedication in raising and homeschooling them, how they saw it was integral to their success.

It's easy to get teary-eyed when I think of those things. I'll always be grateful for knowing that our ten-plus years of learning at home became something much, much bigger.

> **Eden**: A positive outcome of homeschooling that I often take for granted is the close relationship I have with my brother. Because we shared, laughed, fought, and grew in respect for each other while we worked side by side, we were each other's best friend growing up.
>
> Even now as adults, when we aren't together, we communicate frequently through text or video chat, invite the other to hang out with our own friends, and always have each other's back. Friendships are wonderful and important, but there's nothing like the irreplaceable bond that Hart and I share.

This list of blessings could be even longer, but what pleases me most is not how much we accomplished in those learning days or even how early we started schooling. It's that we had precious time together.

If someone asked me if I thought our children would be who they are today without being homeschooled, my answer would be a definite no. Yes, a lot of things boil down to consistent parenting, maybe even influences from one's background or heritage. But the golden moments we spent together and the impact from homeschooling and everything it imparted went far beyond this for us.

As Eden and Hart learned, they were nurtured and loved. They were given the priceless tools that sparked them to think on their own and crave learning. In high school, they even wanted to take extra classes instead of their allowed spares! They showed what a positive experience homeschooling was, and it never held them back. In fact, they rose far above.

Our children are young for such a short period of time, and they won't always be with us. I'm honored to think I may have contributed, even in a small way, to their creativity, originality, and their future successes.

Do I regret taking the time to nurture our children and put my own career on hold? Not once. God had bestowed us with these two little beings to raise to the best of our ability, and I wanted to cherish every moment that I could with them. The road to publishing a novel included obstacles and frustrations, but I persevered because I firmly believe *everything in its time*.

Looking back to the reasons why we homeschooled, I feel a richness in my heart that these hopes were fulfilled tenfold.

In four words, I'd like to sum up why our homeschooling experience was a success. Love. Creativity. Perseverance. Respect. If you foster even two of these traits, you'll discover how far they'll take you in this adventure.

The following is my favorite verse from the Bible that helped me then—and continues to help me now—with every step I take.

Philippians 4:13: *I can do all things through Christ who gives me strength.*

Lastly, please know you're never alone. Find homeschooling groups, make friends, and treasure your avid supporters. Eden and I will be in your corner, rooting for you!

FREQUENTLY ASKED QUESTIONS

Q: I have three children, ages eight, six, and four. How do I structure teaching when they're all at different stages?

Arlene: Since most of us don't have triplets or quintuplets, in a lot of cases, children are at different stages when you homeschool. I'd set up the youngest with an engaging activity like a matching game or a hands-on, self-correcting learning system. While they're immersed in that, take the time to set up the next youngest with their lesson.

Conversely, the opposite may work in your household. You may find it easier to set up your oldest with a worksheet or lesson, then go down the line to the next eldest. I found, with only a two-year spread between our children, that I could teach the basic rules of a lesson that applied to both.

Math, for example. Adding is straightforward. The younger one won't be working in a book with the same difficulty as the older child, but they can still listen for instructions at the same time.

Also, take advantage of studying select topics together. As I explained earlier, in history, I taught a medieval unit to both Eden and Hart. The same thing applied in science and geography.

The younger ones will grasp what they can and will produce what is developmentally possible. Celebrate this. Working together is ideal for everyone as it promotes cooperative learning, and you, as a teacher, won't be spread thin.

Q: I lack discipline myself. I've tried using idle threats to get my kids to cooperate, even promising things, but they don't listen and won't take me seriously. How do I overcome this?

<u>**Arlene**</u>: The answer isn't easy, but if we're going to homeschool our children, they need to understand that this isn't a pass to goof off just because they're at home. They also need to know and trust that you're in charge. If you cave every time you promise to dole out consequences for bad behavior, you'll need to pull up your bootstraps and let your children see you want this to work and that you mean business.

Two things are key that worked for us. First, we never lied to our children or posed empty threats. They knew they could always—without fail—trust whatever we said. That gained respect from the start. As they grew older and knew the doors were always open for communication, they, in turn, were honest with us.

Secondly, we raised Eden and Hart to understand that *no* meant *no*. We didn't waffle. We didn't threaten. The truth was I couldn't take listening to whiny kids. We've all heard them in the grocery store or at the park. The temper tantrums. The stomping feet.

In all honesty, I never once had this trouble. I didn't do anything magical or radical. On occasion, if our children misbehaved, I'd give them a consequence for not listening. No play time with a friend. No screen time, etc. Most important is that I followed through because once again, they could trust that I meant what I said.

Remember that kid having the temper tantrum? Did you hear the parent threaten to take him out of the store if he didn't stop misbehaving? I've seen this numerous times, and what saddens me is that the parent doesn't live up to his or her warning.

Kids are smart. They know the parent will cave and give them what they're screaming for. They may not fully understand what's happening, but they soon learn who's in control.

I know this is tough. You may not have had an ideal upbringing yourself. You're not alone. But it's never too late. We want the best for our children, remember? That might involve sitting the family down and having a discussion that there are going to be some changes. Lay out the new rules, and remember to stick to them.

Q: Did you have homework?

Eden: As the word implies, all the work we did was "home work," but there was no homework as public school kids understand it. My nights were not spent filling out worksheets or reading assignments for the next day. We worked on our allotment of lessons and exercises each day until they were done. If we didn't complete them, and it was time to move on, we'd just pick it up the next day.

Q: Did you have to take tests?

Eden: Yes, but not the standard pass-or-fail since marks weren't emphasized as they are in school. The tests were more a way of quizzing our knowledge. We would close our books and either answer test questions orally or write them down.

Tests were primarily an effective way of checking if we were ready to move on from a unit. They didn't require prior studying and were often spur of the moment, which made them an accurate assessment of our comprehension level.

Q: What was the best part of being homeschooled?

Eden: At the time, my answer was being able to work comfortably at home, having the freedom to move around, and cuddling my cat whenever I felt like it.

Looking back now, I most appreciate that it was an atmosphere that fostered and promoted a self-motivated desire to learn.

Q: Do you wish you went to public school?

Eden: I was homeschooled up until grade 9, so I did spend all my high school years in the public-school system and experienced both sides of education.

Even though I enjoyed high school, I have no regrets about not having attended elementary school.

Q: How was the transition from homeschool to high school?

Eden: For me, the transition wasn't difficult. My high school brought together kids from many different surrounding towns and elementary schools, so it wasn't like I was the only new face. I was also already active in the community with sports and other events.

Since I started at the beginning of grade 9, the couple days of orientation made me realize that my new classmates were just as unsure of what to expect in high school as I was. We were all starting this journey together.

Not having attended elementary school didn't ostracize me or negatively impact my high school experience in any way. Academically, I felt more than prepared for a lot of the classes. Socially, it was a new place for all my peers as well.

SOCIAL MEDIA LINKS

Website:
www.arlenemcfarlane.com

Facebook:
https://www.facebook.com/ArleneMcFarlaneAuthor/

ABOUT THE AUTHORS

Arlene McFarlane is the *USA Today* bestselling author of the Valentine Beaumont comedy mystery series. She's won and placed in over 30 prestigious contests, including the Chanticleer International Mystery & Mayhem Book Awards, and a Voice Arts nomination for her audiobook, *Murder, Curlers & Cream*. She also enjoys traveling to writing conferences, workshops, and reader events. Before becoming a published author, Arlene's most important calling was in homeschooling her children. It was a rich and rewarding experience, and she loves to encourage others who are considering this path.

Arlene lives with her family in Canada.

Eden McFarlane holds a Bachelor of Arts and a Master of Arts from the University of Waterloo. She double majored in Honors French and Honors English with a specialization in Literature and Rhetoric. She completed her postgrad in French Studies. Eden has worked as a teaching assistant and a research assistant and has won multiple awards for her academic literary dissertations.

Eden loves traveling abroad, but Canada remains her home.

www.ingramcontent.com/pod-product-compliance
Lightning Source LLC
Chambersburg PA
CBHW071507070526
44578CB00001B/464